When Love Ends

Healing and Personal Growth, Volume 1

Arturo José Sánchez Hernández

Published by Arturo José Sánchez Hernández, 2024.

WHEN LOVE ENDS

First edition. November 4, 2024.

ISBN: 979-8230381143

Written by Arturo José Sánchez Hernández.

Table of Contents

PREFACE

The end of a romantic relationship can feel like the end of the world. It's a time of deep sadness, when dreams and hopes fade away, leaving us with a sense of emptiness and confusion. However, it can also be an opportunity for personal growth, a door that opens toward self-discovery and transformation.

As a psychiatrist, I have worked with many people who have experienced the pain of a breakup. Over the years, I have witnessed how grief can feel overwhelming, but I have also seen how, with the right support and a compassionate attitude toward oneself, it is possible to find the light at the end of the tunnel and start anew with renewed strength.

This book, "When Love Ends: A Guide to Healing with Dignity," is designed to accompany you through the healing process. It does not claim to offer quick fixes or magic solutions, but rather invites you to reflect on your experiences, process the pain with calmness, and eventually reconnect with yourself in a genuine and empathetic way. In times like these, dignity is an essential pillar for moving forward without losing our essence.

Throughout these pages, you'll find tools and recommendations to navigate the grief of a breakup with integrity. Each reflection aims to remind you that the most important love is the love you have for yourself. Healing is not an easy or immediate process, but it is a journey that, with patience and kindness toward yourself, will lead you to a new stage full of possibilities.

I hope this book will be a light in the darkness, a reminder that although love may change forms, life remains full of opportunities to feel, grow, and love again.

Every ending carries the potential for a new beginning. Even though everything may seem uncertain and painful right now, remember that within you lies the strength to overcome this moment and build a full, authentic life. Allow yourself to feel every emotion, learn from every experience, and trust that the future will bring new opportunities to love and be happy.

With care, Dr. Arturo José Sánchez Hernández.

The Author.

~~~

TO GET BACK OR NOT TO GET BACK: HOW TO RECOGNIZE IF THE RELATIONSHIP HAS A CHANCE FOR RECONCILIATION

Ending a romantic relationship doesn't always mean that everything is lost. Sometimes, after some time for reflection, the question arises: "Should we give it another try?" This is a delicate topic, as getting back together can be an opportunity to grow together, but it can also lead to more pain. Here are some keys to recognize if the relationship has a chance for reconciliation or if it's better to move forward.

Evaluate the Reasons for the Breakup

The first step in considering the possibility of getting back together is to honestly evaluate the reasons for the breakup. Was it communication problems, irreconcilable differences, or harmful behaviors? If the breakup happened due to external factors or a misunderstanding that can be resolved, there may be a chance. However, if there was abuse, chronic distrust, or a lack of respect, it's safer to move on.

Ask Yourself If Both Have Changed

For reconciliation to succeed, it's crucial that both parties have worked on the issues that led to the breakup. Ask yourself if both you and your ex have grown, changed, and learned from the experience. Without genuine changes and a desire to be better, it's very likely that the relationship will fall back into the same problems as before.

Analyze If the Feelings Are Still Strong and Genuine

It's important to ask yourself if the feelings for the other person are still genuine and if there's a mutual desire to build something together. Sometimes nostalgia or the fear of being alone can lead you to idealize the relationship. Make sure that your desire to get back together comes from love and not from fear or habit.

Assess the Ability to Forgive and Let Go of the Past

Getting back together involves being able to forgive and let go of past mistakes. If either of you can't forgive or if resentment is still present, reconciliation will be difficult. True forgiveness is key to starting fresh without carrying the weight of the past. Ask yourself if you can accept what happened and commit to not bringing up old conflicts.

Maintain Honest and Open Communication

A relationship that has a chance for reconciliation needs a solid foundation of honest communication. If both of you can talk openly about what went wrong, what needs to change, and how you plan to improve, then there's a basis to work on together. However, if communication remains difficult or evasive, the same problems are likely to resurface.

Evaluate If There Is Real Commitment from Both Sides

Reconciliation will only work if both parties are willing to commit and work to improve the relationship. Ask yourself if both of you are ready to make compromises, change harmful behaviors, and build a future together. If only one of you is willing to try, it will be very difficult for the relationship to succeed.

Reflect on the Impact on Your Wellbeing

Finally, evaluate whether getting back with your ex contributes to your emotional wellbeing. Do you feel happier, secure, and at peace with the idea of getting back together? Or do you feel anxiety, fear, and constant doubts? Listen to your emotions, as they will give you clues about whether it's a good decision. A relationship should add to your life and make you feel fulfilled, not drain your energy or cause distress.

FINAL THOUGHTS

Deciding whether or not to get back with an ex is an important decision that requires deep and honest reflection. Don't rush or be swayed solely by emotions in the moment. Take time to evaluate whether the relationship has a solid foundation and if both of you are willing to build something new and better. Remember, your priority should be your own wellbeing and personal growth.

~~~

MYTHS AND REALITIES ABOUT HEARTBREAK: BREAKING DOWN FICTION TO UNDERSTAND THE REALITY OF LOSS

Getting over a breakup is a process full of intense emotions, often influenced by the myths we hear. In this section, we will debunk some of these common myths about heartbreak so that you can have a more realistic and constructive view of how to navigate this stage.

Myth 1: "Time heals everything"

Reality: Time alone isn't enough; your attitude matters too. It's true that time tends to heal wounds, but by itself, it's not enough to overcome a breakup. What really matters is how you choose to face that time. Adopting a positive attitude, seeking emotional support, and working on your personal wellbeing are essential to making time your ally, not just a passive witness to your pain.

Myth 2: "You need to be strong and not cry"

Reality: Crying is a natural part of the healing process. Expressing your emotions isn't a sign of weakness—quite the opposite. Crying allows you to release the pain and begin to accept what happened. Allow yourself to feel without judging yourself. Tears are a step toward healing, and being strong often means embracing your vulnerability.

Myth 3: "You need to forget quickly"

Reality: It's not about forgetting; it's about learning to live with it. Trying to forget someone who was important to you can be very difficult and even counterproductive. Instead of forcing yourself to forget, focus on accepting the situation, learning from the experience, and making space for new projects. The goal isn't to erase the past, but to learn to live with it without it hurting you.

Myth 4: "Replace lost love with a new one quickly"

Reality: Not all voids can be filled with another relationship. Seeking a new relationship to fill the emptiness left by the previous one can lead to toxic situations or repeating past mistakes. It's important to heal first, rediscover who you are, and understand what you need. A new relationship should be a positive addition, not a remedy to avoid the pain.

Myth 5: "Men and women deal with heartbreak differently"

Reality: Each person faces heartbreak in their own way, regardless of gender. The belief that men and women handle pain completely differently can lead to unrealistic expectations. Every human experiences grief uniquely. What matters is finding the tools that help you heal, whether it's talking, writing, engaging in physical activities, or seeking professional help.

Myth 6: "You must avoid thinking about your ex at all costs"

Reality: Thinking about the relationship is part of the acceptance process. Trying to avoid any thought about your ex will only prolong the process. Reflecting on what happened is essential for healing. The key is not to hold onto these thoughts obsessively, but to observe them, accept them, and move forward. Reflection helps you learn and grow.

Myth 7: "You shouldn't show sadness in front of others"

Reality: Expressing your pain is natural and necessary. Showing sadness and vulnerability to others is not a sign of weakness. Talking about your feelings with someone you trust—a friend, family member, or therapist—will help you release the pain and find support. Sadness is a valid emotion and part of the process.

Myth 8: "A breakup is a personal failure"

Reality: Not all relationships are meant to last forever. Ending a relationship doesn't mean you've failed. Relationships are opportunities to learn and grow. Sometimes they just stop working, and that's okay. Viewing a breakup as a learning experience will help you grow and be better prepared for the future.

Myth 9: "You need to be friends with your ex to prove everything is okay"

Reality: Staying friends with your ex isn't always healthy. Some people can be friends with their ex, but that doesn't mean it's the best choice for everyone. Every breakup is different, and it's important to listen to your own emotional needs. If staying in contact with your ex makes it harder for you to recover, it's better to create distance and focus on yourself.

Myth 10: "Your life will never be the same without that person"

Reality: While things may change, your life can be just as full—or even more so. It's common to think that life won't be the same without that person, but that doesn't mean it can't be wonderful. Though change is inevitable, over time, you can rebuild your life, find new passions, and surround yourself with people who bring you happiness. The breakup is just the end of a chapter, not your whole story.

FINAL THOUGHTS

Heartbreak, though painful, gives you the opportunity to grow and get to know yourself better. Debunking these myths will help you approach this time with a more realistic and compassionate attitude toward yourself. There's no perfect guide to getting over a breakup, but what matters is taking each day as an opportunity to move toward healing.

~~~

WHEN LOVE ENDS: HOW TO FACE LOSS WITHOUT GUILT

Ending a relationship is a painful process full of complex emotions. The feeling of loss is often accompanied by a constant search for reasons and someone to blame, but the reality is that some relationships simply come to an end without anyone being at fault. Accepting this reality is essential for healing and moving forward. Here are some ideas on how to face loss without guilt and learn to let go with peace.

Accept That the End of a Relationship Doesn't Mean Failure

One of the most harmful beliefs after a breakup is thinking that the end of a relationship equals failure. Many relationships fulfill their purpose—whether it's helping us grow, teaching us important lessons, or simply allowing us to experience love in its purest form. Just because a relationship ends doesn't mean you or your partner failed. Instead of seeing it as a failure, accept it as a chapter that has come to its natural conclusion.

Understand That Love Changes and Evolves

Love doesn't always stay the same. People change, circumstances change, and sometimes love changes too. That intense love at the beginning can evolve into a calmer affection or even fade away. It's important to understand that these changes are natural and don't mean there's something wrong with you or the other person. Recognizing that love can change will help you accept the end without blaming anyone.

Don't Blame Yourself or the Other Person

After a breakup, it's easy to fall into the trap of blaming yourself or the other person. Often, there is no clear person to blame. Relationships end for many reasons: different goals, lack of compatibility, personal changes, among many others. It's important to understand that blaming yourself or the other person will only add more pain and delay the healing process. Instead of seeking someone to blame, focus on accepting the situation and learning what you can for the future.

Practice Forgiveness and Compassion

Forgiving the other person and, most importantly, forgiving yourself is key to facing loss without guilt. Compassion for yourself and your ex-partner will help you let go of resentment and see the situation with greater clarity and peace. Understanding that both of you did the best you could under the circumstances will allow you to free yourself from guilt and move forward. Compassion doesn't mean ignoring what happened but accepting that you are both human and that everyone makes mistakes.

Reflect on the Lessons Learned

Every relationship leaves behind valuable lessons that can help you grow as a person. Reflecting on the lessons from the relationship is a way to make sense of what happened without falling into guilt. Ask yourself what you learned about yourself, your needs, your boundaries, and how you want to relate to others in the future. This approach will help you see the relationship as an important part of your life, but not as a mistake or failure.

Allow Yourself to Feel Without Judgment

It's natural to feel sadness, anger, or even relief after a breakup. All these emotions are valid and necessary for processing the loss. Don't judge yourself for what you feel or for the intensity of your emotions. Allow yourself to cry, talk, write, or express what you're experiencing in whatever way you need. Accepting and expressing your emotions is an important part of the healing process.

Focus on the Future

Accepting that a relationship has ended also means allowing yourself to look forward. Instead of getting stuck in "what went wrong," focus on what you want your life to look like from now on. Set new goals, surround yourself with supportive people, and focus on activities that make you happy. Focusing on the future will help you let go of the past and build a path full of new opportunities.

FINAL THOUGHTS

Understanding that love can end without anyone being at fault is an important step in healing after a breakup. Relationships are experiences that help us grow and are not always meant to last forever. Accepting the end without guilt will allow you to close that chapter of your life with peace and open yourself to new possibilities. Remember, the value of a relationship is not measured by its duration but by what it meant and what you learned from it.

~~~

STAGES OF HEARTBREAK: NAVIGATING THE PAIN WITH HOPE

A breakup can feel like the world is falling apart, taking us through a whirlwind of intense and sometimes conflicting emotions. This process, known as heartbreak, involves different stages that, though painful, are necessary to heal and find peace again. Let's explore these stages and some strategies for getting through them.

DENIAL

Denial is our mind's first response to pain. In this stage, it can be hard to accept that the relationship is over. You might still be hoping for a message, a call, or even fantasizing about a reconciliation. Denial protects us from the pain initially, but it's important to be aware of this phase so that you can move forward.

Recommendation: Try to accept reality little by little. Talk to trusted people about what happened, as expressing your feelings will help you come to terms with the situation.

ANGER

Once reality starts to sink in, anger can arise. You may feel angry at yourself, at the other person, or at life in general. This anger can take many forms—resentment, blame, or irritability without apparent reason. It's normal to feel angry, but channeling it in a healthy way is crucial to not getting stuck in this stage.

Recommendation: Find ways to release this anger constructively, such as physical exercise, journaling, or talking with friends. It's important not to direct this anger at yourself or others.

BARGAINING

In the bargaining stage, you try to make sense of what happened. Thoughts like "What if I had done things differently?" or "What if we give it another chance?" may come up. Here, your mind looks for ways to reverse what happened, as if you could go back in time and change the outcome.

Recommendation: Remember that there is no use in punishing yourself with thoughts of what could have been. Accept that no matter how much you wish it, the past cannot be changed. Instead, focus on what you can learn from the experience for your future.

DEPRESSION

This is the stage where the pain feels the deepest. It may seem like the emptiness will never go away and that the sadness is endless. It's common to feel lonely, unmotivated, or lose interest in things that used to make you happy. It's important to remember that this stage, though difficult, will also pass.

Recommendation: Don't isolate yourself. Allow yourself to feel the pain, but look for activities that bring you comfort, such as spending time with friends and family, practicing hobbies you enjoy, or even seeking professional help if you feel you need it.

ACCEPTANCE

Acceptance doesn't mean you stop feeling pain, but rather that you begin to understand and accept that the relationship has ended. You start to let go of expectations and the "what ifs." Little by little, the sadness transforms into a sense of peace, and you begin to see a more hopeful future.

Recommendation: At this stage, it's time to think about yourself and what you want for your life. Resume personal goals, make new plans, and focus on activities that bring you satisfaction. Each step, no matter how small, will lead you to a better version of yourself.

FINAL THOUGHTS

Heartbreak is a process that takes time, and each person experiences it differently. There is no right way to feel or a specific timeline for getting through each stage. What matters is to be kind to yourself and allow yourself to feel every emotion without rushing. Although the pain may be intense now, over time, you will heal and rebuild your life. You are not alone on this journey!

~~~

ACCEPTING THE PAIN: A NECESSARY STEP IN THE HEALING PROCESS

After understanding the stages of grief, it is important to talk about an essential step that we often avoid: accepting the pain. The end of a relationship can be a devastating experience, and the pain that comes with it is real and profound. However, the path to recovery begins with accepting that pain, recognizing it as a natural part of the healing process.

Pain as a Necessary Part of the Process

Feeling pain is not easy. Often, we want to avoid it, distract ourselves, and move on without facing it. However, the pain after a breakup is a natural response to losing someone important to us. Accepting the pain does not mean giving in to suffering, but rather acknowledging that the sadness is a reflection of the love and significance that relationship had in our life.

When we avoid pain, we only postpone healing. Trying to fill the void with activities, relationships, or distractions only provides temporary relief. Accepting the pain allows us to process what we feel, transform it, and ultimately overcome it.

How to Accept the Pain

– **Allow Yourself to Feel:** To accept the pain, the first thing you need to do is allow yourself to feel. If you need to cry, do it. If you feel sadness, let it flow without judging yourself. Emotions are a part of us, and repressing them only prolongs the process. Feeling is part of healing, and although it may be difficult, it is the first step toward emotional freedom.

– **Don't Fight Against Your Emotions:** Often, we feel guilty for what we feel. We think we should "be okay" faster or that showing sadness is a sign of weakness. However, fighting against our emotions only intensifies the suffering. Stop fighting the pain, and instead, treat it like a guest. Recognize that it is there for a reason and that it is a natural step in the recovery process.

– **Use the Pain as a Tool for Growth:** Even though it may seem impossible in the moment, pain can be a powerful tool for personal growth. Ask yourself: What can I learn from this experience? How can I use this difficult time to become stronger and know myself better? Pain teaches us about our needs, our boundaries, and our values. Using it as a catalyst for growth can help give new meaning to the suffering.

– **Find a Safe Space to Express What You Feel:** Talking to someone you trust about how you feel, writing in a journal, or engaging in artistic activities that allow you to express your pain are effective ways to accept what you are going through. The act of expressing yourself is liberating and will help you process your emotions in a healthier way.

– **Remember That Pain Is Temporary:** Although it may seem like the pain will last forever during the hardest moments, it is important to remember that all pain is temporary. Acceptance does not mean that the pain will stay forever, but rather that it is a way to face it without running away. Time, along with acceptance, is the best ally for the pain to lessen and for you to find peace again.

The Power of Accepting the Pain

Accepting the pain is an act of courage and self-love. It is not always easy to face what we feel, but when we do, we give ourselves the chance to truly heal. Pain is a part of life, and though we often try to avoid it, it is also what allows us to grow, evolve, and find deeper meaning in our experiences.

FINAL THOUGHTS

Accepting the pain after a breakup does not mean giving in to it, but giving it the space it needs to be processed and transformed. Remember that pain is just another stage in the healing process, and through acceptance, you can find the strength needed to rebuild yourself. Give the pain the welcome it deserves, and little by little, you will see it become the fertile ground for new beginnings and a stronger version of yourself.

~~~

THE VALUE OF TIME TO HEAL: THE IMPORTANCE OF GIVING SPACE FOR RECOVERY

Ending a relationship can be one of the most challenging emotional experiences to face. Amid the pain, it is natural to feel the urge to find quick relief, to fill the void with a new relationship, or to seek distractions that minimize the suffering. However, the true healing process requires time and care. Here, I will discuss the importance of giving yourself the time needed to heal and how to avoid rushing to fill that void with another relationship.

Time to Heal: An Act of Self-Love

Taking the time to heal is a gift you give to yourself. Allowing yourself space to process the pain, reflect on what happened, and understand your own emotions better is an act of self-love. By doing so, you reconnect with yourself, understand what you need, and determine what you want for the future. Healing is not a linear process, and it's okay to have good days and not-so-good days. What's important is to allow yourself to feel and not pressure yourself to "be okay" right away.

Learning from the Experience

A breakup is not just the end of a chapter but also an opportunity to learn. Giving yourself time to heal involves reflecting on what worked and what didn't in the relationship and learning from those experiences to grow and avoid repeating harmful patterns. When you rush into a new relationship, you risk repeating the same mistakes because you haven't taken the time to reflect and learn. The value of time to heal lies in being able to turn the pain into wisdom.

Avoid Filling the Void with Another Relationship

It's common to think that a new relationship will help you get over the previous one, but this can be a temporary fix that does not address the root of the issue. Relationships that start to avoid pain or loneliness are often unhealthy, as they do not come from a place of fulfillment but from a place of need. Instead of looking for someone else to fill the void, focus on healing and rebuilding your life from emotional independence. That way, when you are ready for a new relationship, you can enter it from a place of wellbeing, without depending on the other person to feel complete.

Face the Pain Instead of Avoiding It

Feeling the pain of a breakup is not easy, but it is an essential part of the healing process. Pain is a signal that something significant has changed, and facing it will allow you to overcome it over time. Avoiding the pain, whether by seeking a new relationship or constant distractions, may seem easier initially, but in the long run, unprocessed pain can manifest in other ways, such as anxiety, insecurity, or problems in future relationships. Allowing yourself to feel the pain, cry, talk, and seek emotional support is what will eventually help you heal.

Reconnect with Your Interests and Passions

The time after a breakup is also an opportunity to reconnect with what makes you happy. Use this time to explore your interests, rediscover passions you may have set aside, and take care of your physical and mental wellbeing. Practicing a hobby, exercising, traveling, reading, or simply spending time with loved ones will help you rediscover who you are outside of the relationship and regain a sense of fulfillment in your life.

Build a Solid Emotional Foundation for the Future

Taking time to heal not only has a positive impact on the present but also on the future. By healing consciously, you are building a stronger emotional foundation for future relationships. You will be better prepared to establish healthy boundaries, communicate effectively, and recognize what you truly want and need in a partner. A new relationship should add to your life, not serve as a cure for past wounds.

FINAL THOUGHTS

Healing after a breakup is a process that requires time, patience, and a lot of self-love. There are no shortcuts or magic formulas to avoid the pain, but giving yourself the time you need is the best way to ensure that the pain eventually transforms into growth. By taking care of yourself and avoiding the rush to fill the void with a new relationship, you are building a healthier future full of possibilities.

~~~

THE IMPORTANCE OF LETTING GO: RELEASE TO MOVE FORWARD

Letting go of someone we once loved is one of the most challenging but important processes we can face. It is not just about accepting the end of a relationship but also about learning to live with memories without letting them hurt us. Here, we reflect on why letting go is crucial for personal growth and emotional wellbeing.

Acceptance Is the First Step

Accepting that the relationship has ended is key to beginning the healing process. It is normal to feel resistance; after all, no one likes to lose something that once made them happy. But accepting reality is a sign of emotional strength and maturity. It allows us to face the present with honesty and opens the door to new opportunities.

Memories Don't Have to Be Painful

The memories of a relationship can sometimes feel like daggers to the heart, especially right after a breakup. However, it is possible to change the way we relate to these memories. Instead of letting them cause us pain, we can see them as part of our story—valuable experiences that helped shape who we are today. Over time, those memories can become reminders of love and growth rather than loss.

Letting Go Doesn't Mean Forgetting

Letting go is often misunderstood as forgetting. But it doesn't mean erasing someone from our life; it means releasing the emotional attachment and expectations that keep us tied to the past. We can honor what we had without feeling obligated to hold onto it forever. This process frees us from resentment and allows us to move forward with greater peace.

The Power of Self-Love

When we let go, we also make space to reconnect with ourselves. Self-love becomes our anchor, reminding us of our worth and helping us heal. Taking care of our emotional and physical needs becomes the priority, giving us the strength to embrace the future with confidence.

Creating New Paths

Letting go allows us to create new paths and open our hearts to new possibilities. It is about shifting our focus from what we have lost to what we can gain. By releasing the past, we make space for new relationships, experiences, and opportunities that better align with who we are now and who we want to become.

FINAL THOUGHTS

Letting go is a brave act of self-care. It means choosing to live without the weight of what no longer serves us and allowing ourselves to heal, grow, and transform. Learning to live with memories without letting them cause pain is an important step toward emotional freedom and future happiness.

~~~

SELF-CARE AFTER A BREAKUP: RECOMMENDATIONS TO HEAL MIND AND BODY

A breakup can be one of the most difficult moments in life, and the emotional impact can affect every aspect of your wellbeing. However, it is precisely in these moments that you need to take care of yourself the most. Here, I share some suggestions for taking care of your physical and mental health after a separation, helping you heal and rediscover your inner strength.

Exercise: Activate Your Body and Release Tension

Exercise is a powerful tool for dealing with stress and sadness. When you move, your body releases endorphins, known as the "happiness hormones," which help improve your mood. Whether it's going for a run, dancing, practicing yoga, or taking walks in nature, physical activity will help you release tension and feel better about yourself. Additionally, exercise allows you to disconnect from negative thoughts and focus on something positive for your health.

Meditation and Mindfulness: Find Peace in the Present

A breakup can create a rollercoaster of thoughts and emotions that can be overwhelming. Meditation and mindfulness can help reduce anxiety and find some calm amid the chaos. Spend a few minutes each day practicing meditation, focusing on your breath and observing your thoughts without judgment. This will help you process your emotions and reduce stress, connecting you more with the present and less with worries about the past or future.

Healthy Eating: Nourish Your Body to Feel Better

During a breakup, it's common to lose your appetite or seek comfort in unhealthy foods. However, good nutrition plays a crucial role in your emotional wellbeing. Try to maintain a balanced diet rich in fruits, vegetables, lean proteins, and healthy fats. Foods like nuts, avocados, and fish are rich in omega-3 and help improve mood. Remember that nourishing your body is also a way to nourish your mind and keep your energy at optimal levels.

Adequate Rest: The Importance of Good Sleep

Adequate rest is essential for emotional recovery. During a breakup, sadness and anxiety can often affect your sleep quality, but making an effort to maintain a healthy sleep routine can make a big difference. Try to sleep at least 7-8 hours each night and establish a relaxing bedtime routine, such as reading a book, listening to soft music, or practicing relaxation techniques. Sleeping well will help you have more mental clarity and better handle your emotions.

Express Your Emotions: Don't Bottle Everything Up

It is important to make space for your emotions and allow yourself to feel without judgment. Talking with friends, writing in a journal, or seeking professional support can be very helpful for releasing your feelings. Grief after a breakup is completely normal, and talking about how you feel will help you process the situation in a healthier way. Don't be afraid to ask for help if you feel you need it—emotional support from others is key in this process.

Dedicate Time to Your Passions and New Projects

After a breakup, it is a good time to reconnect with your passions or explore new activities. Engaging in a hobby you enjoy, such as painting, cooking, reading, or learning something new, will help you feel more productive and enjoy quality time with yourself. You can also set small personal goals that motivate you to move forward, as this will help you focus on the positive and leave behind negative thoughts.

Surround Yourself with Positive People

Social support is essential during the healing process. Surround yourself with friends and family who bring you positive energy and make you feel good. Spending time with people who care about you will help you remember that you are not alone and that you have a support network. Plan activities with friends that make you laugh and enjoy the present. Connection with others is a powerful source of comfort and joy during difficult times.

Establish New Routines: Create a Sense of Stability

A breakup can make you feel like your life has lost stability. Creating new daily routines can help you feel more in control and find a sense of security. Set schedules for your meals, exercise, relaxation time, and sleep. These new routines will help you focus on yourself and create a healthy environment where you can heal.

FINAL THOUGHTS

After a breakup, taking care of your physical and mental health is a priority. Through exercise, meditation, healthy eating, and surrounding yourself with positive support, you can begin to heal and rediscover your strength. Remember that the process takes time and that every small step counts. Allow yourself to feel, heal, and grow, and be assured that you are on the right path to becoming a stronger and happier version of yourself.

~~~

EMOTIONAL CARE: PRACTICAL STRATEGIES FOR HEALING AFTER A BREAKUP

Healing after a breakup isn't just about taking care of our bodies; it's also about caring for our emotions. While it's common to focus on physical self-care, like getting enough rest and eating well, it's equally important to pay attention to our emotional wellbeing.

Why Is Emotional Care Important?

When we go through the process of heartbreak, our emotions can be intense and overwhelming. We may feel sadness, anxiety, anger, confusion—and all of these emotions are valid. Emotional care involves attending to these feelings, accepting that they are there, and allowing ourselves to process them in a healthy way. By paying attention to our emotional wellbeing, we are taking essential steps toward healing.

Strategies for Emotional Care

Here are some specific strategies that can help you take care of yourself emotionally and ease the healing process:

Breathing Techniques

Deep breathing is one of the most effective ways to calm the nervous system. When anxiety or pain feels too intense, try the following technique:

– Inhale deeply through your nose while counting to 4.

– Hold the air in your lungs while counting to 4.

– Exhale slowly through your mouth while counting to 6.

– Repeat the cycle several times until you feel your body relax.

This technique helps reduce stress, relieve anxiety, and bring calmness to the present moment.

Meditation

Meditation can be a great ally in navigating pain. You don't need to be an expert to benefit from it. Just find a quiet place, sit comfortably, and focus your attention on your breath. At first, your mind may wander, and that's okay. Over time, you'll learn to observe your thoughts without judging them and allow them to pass.

Practicing mindfulness can help you accept your emotions without feeling overwhelmed by them and give you a greater sense of control over your mind and body.

Therapeutic Writing

Writing about how you feel can be a powerful tool for processing pain. You can start each day by jotting down your thoughts, your feelings, or simply what happened during the day. Writing is a way to get out what's inside, to release emotions, and to better understand what you're experiencing.

Here are some ideas to get started:

– Write a letter that you will never send to the person you have parted from.

– Note three things you are grateful for each day (yes, even in the midst of pain, there is always something to be grateful for).

– Keep a journal where you allow yourself to be honest without restrictions.

Positive Visualizations

Visualize a place that brings you peace, a space where you feel safe. It could be a real or imaginary landscape. Close your eyes and try to recreate that place in your mind—the colors, the sounds, the weather. This practice can help you find an internal refuge when the pain becomes overwhelming.

How These Tools Can Help You Heal

Emotional care is not about avoiding pain but facing it with love and patience. By incorporating breathing techniques, meditation, writing, and visualization into your routine, you'll be giving yourself the space and tools needed to process your emotions in a way that allows you to grow and move forward.

As you heal, remember that you are not alone in this process. We all face pain in different ways, and caring for yourself emotionally is an act of courage and self-love.

FINAL THOUGHTS

Taking care of our emotional wellbeing after a breakup is not a luxury—it is a necessity. Healing starts from within, and every step you take to address your emotions is a step toward rebuilding your inner peace. Breathe, meditate, write, and keep moving forward. Every tool you use is a sign of the love you have for yourself.

~~~

THE ROLE OF FAMILY AND FRIENDS IN OVERCOMING A BREAKUP: LEANING ON YOUR LOVED ONES

A breakup can be one of the hardest experiences to face. The pain, sadness, and uncertainty can feel overwhelming, but you don't have to go through this process alone. Friends and loved ones play a fundamental role in overcoming a breakup, and knowing how to lean on them and ask for the kind of help you need can make a big difference in your healing journey. Here, we will explore how friends can help you through a breakup and how to communicate your needs clearly.

The Value of Social Support

When we go through a breakup, social support becomes one of the most powerful tools for healing. Friends and loved ones offer companionship, comfort, and a different perspective that helps us feel less alone and see the situation from other points of view. Feeling that someone is by our side, willing to listen without judgment, helps us process the pain and remember that we are not alone in our experience.

Social support is not only emotionally valuable but also has positive effects on our mental and physical health. Studies have shown that people with a good social support system tend to recover faster from stressful events and are less likely to develop symptoms of anxiety and depression. The feeling of belonging and emotional support acts as a buffer against pain, and friends can be a crucial pillar during these difficult times.

Different Ways Friends Can Help You

Not all friends offer the same type of support, and it is important to understand that each one has their own way of helping. Some ways in which your friends can be of help include:

- **Listening Without Judgment:** Having someone who listens while you express your thoughts and emotions is invaluable. Sometimes, you just need to vent and share how you feel without receiving advice, and friends who know how to listen can provide that safe space.

- **Distracting You From the Pain:** Other friends may offer you distractions. Planning an outing, going to the movies, playing a sport together, or simply spending a fun afternoon is a great way to disconnect from the sadness and focus on something positive. Distraction is also useful for avoiding obsessive negative thoughts or easing loneliness.

– **Offering an Objective Perspective:** Sometimes, we need someone to help us see things from a more objective perspective. Friends can be that voice reminding us that, although the pain is intense now, it won't last forever, and they can help us understand that the breakup was for the best. An outside perspective can be key to finding clarity and starting to accept the situation.

– **Practical Support:** Some friends can also help you with practical things. Whether it's accompanying you to do errands, helping you move, or just being there for those everyday tasks that seem more difficult when you're grieving, their practical support is essential. These acts of kindness remind you that you have people you can rely on who are willing to help you through tough times.

– **Emotional Validation:** Validation is essential for processing the emotions of a breakup. Friends who validate your feelings allow you to feel without minimizing or judging them. They remind you that it's okay to feel sadness, anger, or even relief. Knowing that what you feel is normal and that you're not alone in your emotions gives you the strength to move forward.

How to Ask for the Support You Need

Sometimes, our friends want to help us, but they don't know exactly how. That's why it's important to communicate clearly what kind of support you need. Here are some tips on how to ask for help effectively:

– **Be Clear About Your Needs:** Don't be afraid to tell your friends what you need. If you just want someone to listen without giving advice, say so. If you need to go out and distract yourself, communicate that as well. Being clear about your needs will make it easier for your friends to help you in the best way. Being specific allows your friends to know how to act and respond in a way that truly helps you.

– **Set Boundaries:** At times, you may want to be alone, and that's okay. Communicate these boundaries to your friends in a kind way so they know when to give you space and when you're ready to receive their company. Sometimes, you need time alone to process what you're feeling, and your friends need to understand and respect those moments. Setting clear and healthy boundaries will help make the support effective without feeling overwhelmed.

– **Appreciate Their Support:** Showing gratitude to your friends for their support is important. Thanking them for being there for you will not only strengthen your relationship but also make them feel like they're truly helping. A simple "thank you for listening" can have a big impact. Gratitude also contributes to a positive environment and strengthens the bond of friendship.

Surround Yourself with Positive People

It is crucial to surround yourself with people who bring you positive energy during this process. Sometimes, well-intentioned friends may make comments that are not helpful or that make you feel worse. In those cases, it is better to prioritize time with friends who truly bring you calm, joy, and unconditional support.

Positive people will not only help you feel better but also motivate you to engage in activities that promote your wellbeing, like going for a walk, trying a new hobby, or simply having conversations that make you laugh. Surround yourself with those who help you see the best in yourself and remind you of your value, even if the relationship has ended.

The Importance of Not Isolating Yourself

One common reaction after a breakup is wanting to isolate yourself and avoid others. While it is natural to want some time to process emotions, prolonged isolation can make healing more difficult. Friends and loved ones can be a beacon of light during those dark times, helping you stay connected to the world and reminding you that life goes on.

Participating in social activities, even if you don't always feel completely ready, can help you feel better. You don't have to make big plans; even simple activities like having coffee with a friend or taking a walk in the park can make a big difference in your mood. Connection with others is one of the most effective ways to combat sadness and feel like you are still part of the world around you.

The Importance of Collective Self-Care

Your friends can also be a great support in encouraging self-care. Practicing self-care activities together, like exercising, cooking a healthy meal, or attending a yoga class, can be an excellent way to strengthen your physical and mental wellbeing during the grieving process. Collective self-care not only keeps you focused on yourself but also creates moments of positive connection with your friends, reinforcing the importance of mutual support.

Participating in activities that make you feel well accompanied also reminds you that you don't have to face the healing process alone. You can lean on your group of friends to share self-care experiences and create a routine that helps you cope with the pain of the breakup.

FINAL THOUGHTS

Overcoming a breakup is a process that can be long and painful, but you don't have to do it alone. Leaning on your friends and loved ones will help you feel understood, accompanied, and supported during those difficult moments. Clearly communicating your needs, surrounding yourself with positive people, and allowing yourself to be vulnerable with those who care about you is essential for healing. Remember, the support of others will not only help you overcome the breakup but also remind you of your worth and how many people are by your side.

~~~

REDISCOVERING YOURSELF AFTER A BREAKUP: AN OPPORTUNITY TO RECONNECT WITH YOUR PASSIONS

A breakup can be painful and difficult, but it can also become an opportunity to look inward and rediscover who you are. Amid the pain, we can forget that every loss also brings with it the possibility of a new connection with ourselves. Below, I show you how a breakup can be the beginning of a journey toward self-rediscovery and how you can use this moment to reconnect with your passions and interests.

Take a Pause to Reflect

A breakup leaves us with time and space to reflect on what we want in life, what makes us happy, and what we need to change. This is a good moment to pause, breathe, and look inward. Ask yourself: What activities or interests did you have before the relationship? What things did you set aside that you would like to take up again? This reflection is an essential first step in rediscovering what excites you and reconnecting with yourself.

Reconnect with Your Hobbies and Favorite Activities

During a relationship, we sometimes set aside our hobbies and interests to accommodate the needs and preferences of our partner. Now is the time to reclaim them. Whether it's painting, cooking, reading, playing a sport, or learning something new, dedicating time to those hobbies is a great way to reconnect with what makes you happy. It will not only help distract you and make you feel better, but it will also remind you of the things that have always excited you and bring you fulfillment.

Discover New Passions

It's not just about taking up past activities; a breakup is also an opportunity to explore new things. Take advantage of this time to experiment, to try activities you've always wanted to do but never had the time or motivation for. You could learn to play an instrument, go hiking, take cooking classes, or even try yoga or meditation. Exploring new passions will not only help keep your mind occupied but also help you grow and discover new ways to enjoy life.

Reconnect with Friends and Family

Romantic relationships can consume a lot of our time and energy, which is natural, but sometimes we neglect other important relationships. Now is the time to reconnect with your friends and family, to spend time with them, and to strengthen those bonds that have always been a part of your life. Surround yourself with people who make you feel good, who support you, and who help you remember who you are outside of the relationship. The support of your loved ones is an important part of the rediscovery process.

Dedicate Time to Self-Care

Self-care is essential in the process of rediscovery. Take time to care for yourself, both physically and emotionally. You could create an exercise routine you enjoy, cook healthy meals, practice meditation to calm your mind, or take a relaxing bath after a long day. Self-care not only helps you heal but also reminds you how important you are and that you deserve your own love and attention.

Set New Personal Goals

A breakup can also be an opportunity to reassess your goals and aspirations. Reflect on what you want to achieve from now on. It could be a good time to focus on your career, your health, or a personal project you've always wanted to start. Setting new goals and working towards them will give you purpose and help you focus on yourself, your growth, and your personal achievements. It is an excellent way to transform pain into motivation.

Learn to Enjoy Your Own Company

Being alone doesn't have to mean being lonely. In fact, learning to enjoy your own company is one of the best ways to grow and rediscover yourself after a breakup. Take advantage of this time to do activities you enjoy on your own: a walk outdoors, an afternoon watching your favorite movies, or simply a moment of reflection and tranquility. Finding satisfaction in being with yourself is a sign of personal growth and strength.

FINAL THOUGHTS

A breakup can be painful, but it can also be the beginning of a beautiful journey toward rediscovering who you are and what you love. Don't be afraid to explore, reconnect with what has always made you happy, and open yourself up to new possibilities. Remember that every ending is also a new beginning, and this can be your moment to flourish and become the best version of yourself.

~~~

BREAKUP AND SELF-CONFIDENCE: HOW TO REBUILD YOUR SELF-ESTEEM

Breakups not only sever emotional ties but can also leave deep wounds in our self-confidence. It's normal to feel your self-esteem waver after a separation, as negative thoughts and self-doubt can take over. However, this can also be a pivotal moment to rebuild, reconnect, and strengthen your sense of self. Below, I share some strategies to help you regain your self-esteem and come out stronger from this process.

Understand That the End of a Relationship Does Not Define Your Worth

A breakup can make you feel like you're not enough or that something is wrong with you. It's important to remember that the end of a relationship does not define your worth as a person. Relationships end for a wide variety of reasons, and many of those reasons have nothing to do with your personal value. Learn to differentiate the value of the relationship from your own value as an individual. You are so much more than a relationship that didn't work out.

Accept Your Emotions Without Judgment

It's common to experience a rollercoaster of emotions after a breakup: sadness, anger, relief, nostalgia. All of these emotions are valid and necessary to process the separation. Accept how you feel without judging yourself. Crying, feeling frustrated, or even having days when you don't feel okay is part of the process. Allow yourself to experience these emotions, as their acceptance is the first step to start healing and rebuilding your self-confidence.

Reconnect With What Makes You Happy

After a breakup, it's a good time to reconnect with your passions and personal interests. Sometimes, in a relationship, we put aside certain activities that made us happy. Getting back to those hobbies or exploring new interests will help you remember what makes you unique and valuable. Whether it's painting, dancing, playing a sport, or learning something new, dedicating time to yourself is an excellent way to strengthen your self-esteem.

Talk to Yourself With Kindness

After a breakup, it's easy to fall into the habit of self-criticism and negative self-talk: "I wasn't enough," "I always fail in relationships." These thoughts undermine your confidence. Change that inner dialogue and talk to yourself as you would to a good friend. Be kind and compassionate. Remind yourself of your qualities, your achievements, and what makes you a good person. Speaking to yourself with kindness is key to rebuilding your self-confidence.

Set Small, Realistic Goals

Self-confidence grows when we fulfill our own promises and goals. After a breakup, set small, realistic goals that you can achieve, such as exercising three times a week, learning something new, or meditating every day. Each time you achieve one of these goals, you'll feel that you can trust yourself and your ability to move forward. These small accomplishments will help you regain a sense of control and remind you of your ability to overcome challenges.

Surround Yourself With Supportive People

Social support is essential during the process of healing and rebuilding self-confidence. Seek out friends and family who listen, support, and encourage you to see your worth. Surround yourself with people who make you feel good and avoid those who criticize or make you feel less. Feeling the love and support of those around you is fundamental to rebuilding your self-esteem.

Let Go of Comparison

It's easy to fall into the trap of comparing yourself to others, especially when dealing with the pain of a breakup. You may think that others seem to be in perfect relationships or that your ex is getting over the breakup faster than you are. However, comparison only diminishes your self-esteem. Focus on your own path and remember that everyone has their own process and pace. Value your progress, even if it's small, and avoid comparing yourself to others.

Recognize Your Worth Outside of a Relationship

Your worth does not depend on being in a relationship. You are a complete and valuable person on your own, regardless of whether you are in a relationship or not. Sometimes, we believe that our self-esteem is tied to having a partner, but it's important to recognize that self-love is the most important love you can cultivate. Acknowledge your qualities, celebrate your achievements, and find satisfaction in being who you are.

FINAL THOUGHTS

A breakup can shake our self-confidence, but it can also be an opportunity to rebuild and grow stronger. Remember that this is a process that takes time, and it's normal to feel ups and downs along the way. With patience, kindness, and proper care, you can regain and strengthen your self-esteem, rediscovering just how valuable you truly are.

~~~

THE RELATIONSHIP BETWEEN HEARTBREAK AND PERSONAL GROWTH: TURNING PAIN INTO A CATALYST FOR CHANGE

A breakup can be one of the most painful experiences in life, but it can also be one of the most transformative opportunities. When we go through heartbreak, it's easy to feel lost and vulnerable, but this process also provides a great opportunity to grow and improve aspects of ourselves. Below, we explore how breakups can become a catalyst for personal growth and how to use this moment to rediscover and strengthen your life.

Connect With Your Emotions and Know Yourself Better

Heartbreak involves a whirlwind of emotions: sadness, anger, loneliness, nostalgia, among others. While these emotions can seem overwhelming, they also represent an opportunity to connect with yourself in a deep and sincere way. Allowing your emotions to be expressed without judgment will help you know yourself better, understand your needs, and discover aspects of yourself that you hadn't explored before. This process will give you a deeper understanding of who you are and what you truly want in your life.

Rediscover Your Independence

When we're in a relationship, it's normal for some parts of our lives to blend with our partner's. After a breakup, you have the opportunity to rediscover your independence and remember what makes you unique. You can take advantage of this time to pick up activities you used to enjoy, dedicate time to your favorite hobbies, and rediscover what you're passionate about. The breakup becomes an opportunity to explore who you are outside of the relationship and to strengthen your sense of identity.

Learn From Past Mistakes

Every relationship, regardless of how it ended, has valuable lessons to offer. Reflecting on what worked and what didn't in your past relationship can help you learn from your mistakes and grow. What could you have done differently? What aspects would you like to improve in future relationships? Using this moment to learn about yourself and how you relate to others is an excellent way to grow and prepare for healthier, more fulfilling relationships in the future.

Strengthen Your Resilience

Going through a breakup can make you feel like your world is falling apart, but it's also an opportunity to strengthen your resilience. Emotional pain is one of the hardest tests to overcome, but every day you get up and keep going, you're developing your ability to face adversity. This experience will make you stronger, more capable of handling future challenges, and more confident in yourself. Resilience is a quality developed through challenges, and heartbreak is one of those moments that, although painful, can make you stronger.

Cultivate Self-Love

Heartbreak can also be a great opportunity to work on self-love. Sometimes, in a relationship, we forget to take care of ourselves because we put the other person first. Take this time to prioritize yourself, take care of yourself, and learn to love yourself just as you are. Self-love is the foundation for any healthy relationship, and the stronger your love for yourself, the more prepared you'll be for future relationships. Spend time doing things you enjoy, taking care of your body, and surrounding yourself with people who value you.

Develop New Skills and Goals

After a breakup, you might feel that there's a void in your life, but that void can also be filled with new goals and personal projects. This is a good time to learn something new, whether it's a language, an artistic skill, or something you've always wanted to do but never found the time for. Developing new skills and setting new goals will help you stay focused on something positive, increase your confidence, and grow as a person. It will also provide you with a sense of accomplishment and satisfaction that is essential for personal growth.

Reconsider What You Want in a Relationship

The grieving process also gives you the opportunity to reflect on what you truly want in a relationship. Perhaps in the past, you settled for less than you deserved or weren't clear about the qualities you valued in a partner. Now, you can take the time to define your boundaries, your needs, and the type of relationship you want to build in the future. This reflection will help you have a clearer vision and seek relationships that truly contribute to your happiness and growth.

FINAL THOUGHTS

Heartbreak can be devastating, but it can also be a great opportunity to grow and improve as a person. It's not about forgetting or eliminating the pain immediately but about learning from the experience, connecting with yourself, and working to become a better version of yourself. Remember that every challenge in life can also be an opportunity to move forward, and every step you take toward healing is a step toward a brighter future full of possibilities.

~~~

RELATIONSHIP WITH AN EX: IS FRIENDSHIP POSSIBLE?

After a breakup, a common question arises: "Can we be friends?" The idea of maintaining a friendship with an ex-partner is something many people consider, whether because they still value the other person, feel there is something worth preserving, or believe that transitioning to a friendship could make the separation less painful. However, the answer to this question isn't simple and depends on many personal and emotional factors. In this reflection, we'll explore whether or not it's really advisable to maintain a friendship with an ex.

It Depends on How the Relationship Ended

The first aspect to consider is how the relationship ended. If the breakup was amicable and both decided mutually that separation was the best option, it may be easier to think about a friendship. However, if the relationship ended amid conflicts, betrayals, or resentments, friendship might not be a healthy option. In those cases, it's important to reflect on whether maintaining contact will help you heal or if it will keep reopening old wounds.

Ask Yourself Why You Want to Be Friends With Your Ex

Before deciding whether you want to be friends with your ex, ask yourself why you want to maintain the friendship. Sometimes, the desire to stay friends comes from fear of fully letting go, emotional dependence, or hope that the relationship might be restored at some point. If the motivation for being friends is tied to not being able to accept the end of the relationship, it's likely that the friendship won't be healthy and will end up causing more pain. It's essential to be honest with yourself about your intentions.

Consider the Time Needed to Heal

Time is a crucial factor in the possibility of being friends with an ex. After a breakup, you need a period to process the separation, heal wounds, and reconnect with yourself. Trying to be friends immediately after the breakup can complicate the grieving process and make it harder to overcome lingering feelings. If after a significant amount of time both of you feel that you can be friends without pain or unresolved expectations, then it may be possible.

Is It a Friendship That Truly Adds Value?

A friendship should be something that adds value and well-being to your life. Ask yourself if a friendship with your ex would truly be positive, if it would make you feel good, and if it would help you grow. If maintaining the friendship involves mixed feelings, jealousy, anxiety, or pain, it may be best to take a step back. A true friendship should be based on respect, peace, and mutual support, not on suffering or constant uncertainty.

Consider the Impact on New Relationships

Another important aspect is how a friendship with your ex might affect your future relationships. Some new partners may feel uncomfortable or insecure if you maintain a close relationship with an ex. It's important to think about how this friendship could influence your future relationships and whether you're willing to face potential complications. Being honest and transparent with a future partner about this friendship is key to avoiding misunderstandings and issues.

The Importance of Clear Boundaries

If you decide that you want to try being friends with your ex, it's essential to establish clear boundaries. These boundaries help prevent confusion and protect both of your emotional well-being. Defining what type of contact is appropriate, what topics of conversation should be avoided, and how to handle delicate situations is important for the friendship to be genuinely healthy. Without clear boundaries, it's easy to fall into old patterns and reopen wounds that should have healed.

Accept That It's Not Always Possible

Finally, it's important to accept that it's not always possible or advisable to be friends with an ex. Some relationships leave deep wounds, and ongoing contact only makes the healing process harder. In other cases, the differences are so significant that friendship simply isn't viable. And that's okay. Not everyone is meant to stay in our lives forever, and learning to let go is also a fundamental part of personal and emotional growth.

FINAL THOUGHTS

Being friends with an ex-partner is a question that doesn't have a universal answer. Each situation is unique, and the possibility of friendship depends on how the relationship ended, both people's intentions, the time needed to heal, and whether the friendship truly adds something positive to your lives. The most important thing is to be honest with yourself and prioritize your emotional well-being. If friendship with an ex brings you peace, respect, and joy, then it may be worth trying. But if it only brings confusion, anxiety, or pain, it's better to move on.

~~~

BREAKUP AND SOCIAL MEDIA: HOW TO AVOID ADDITIONAL HARM

Ending a relationship is a difficult process, and in the age of social media, this challenge can become even more complicated. Today, deciding whether to maintain or break contact on digital platforms not only influences our emotional recovery but can also turn our social media into sources of suffering or spaces for healing. Here are some key strategies to protect your emotional well-being and avoid further harm during this process.

Evaluate Social Media Contact

It's normal to feel curious about your ex's life, but continuing to see them online can increase your pain. Blocking, unfollowing, or limiting the visibility of their posts can give you the personal space you need to heal.

Avoid Emotional or Impulsive Posts

Social media allows us to express ourselves, but during times of pain, it's better to avoid posting messages that could be misinterpreted or that you might regret. Remember that sharing indirect messages or emotionally charged thoughts only makes things worse and complicates your recovery. Think twice before posting.

Resist the Temptation to "Stalk"

Checking on what your ex is doing may give a false sense of connection, but it only hinders your healing process. If you feel tempted to view their profile or look into their current life, remember that this behavior hurts you and feeds negative emotions like anger or sadness. Protect your emotional peace by avoiding these behaviors.

Establish an Offline Routine

Spending less time on social media will help you focus on yourself and your interests. Get involved in activities that bring you peace and satisfaction outside the digital environment. Enjoying an active life and present moments will allow you to recharge your energy and discover things that truly motivate you.

Surround Yourself With Positive Support

Seek out friends and family who inspire and support you during this time. Use your social networks to interact with positive content and avoid anything that reminds you of the breakup. Over time, you'll notice that the company of those who care about you is key to building a solid foundation in this new phase.

Practice "Digital No Contact" if Necessary

In some breakups, continuous contact is counterproductive, as it delays healing. Consider a period of "digital no contact" to give yourself the space you need. This not only protects your emotions but also allows you to focus on your recovery and personal growth.

Make Your Profile a Safe and Positive Space

Refresh your profile and fill it with content that inspires you and makes you feel good. Post about your achievements, projects, or new activities—not to pretend, but to feel comfortable and empowered in your digital space.

FINAL THOUGHTS

Getting over a breakup in the age of social media has its challenges, but with proper boundaries and a mindful use of these platforms, you can avoid a lot of unnecessary pain. Remember that protecting your peace is the most important thing, and every step you take to safeguard your emotions brings you closer to healing.

~~~

SUGGESTIONS FOR GETTING OVER A BREAKUP WITHOUT LOSING YOUR DIGNITY: STAY CALM AND COMPOSED

Getting over a breakup is a challenge that can test our dignity and self-esteem. However, it is possible to face this process with maturity and respect, both for yourself and for the other person. Here are some suggestions for handling the separation without losing your dignity.

Accept Your Emotions

During a breakup, it's natural to feel sadness, anger, or fear. Allow yourself to feel these emotions without judgment. Recognizing them is the first step toward healing.

Set Clear Boundaries

It's essential to establish healthy boundaries with the other person. Avoid situations where you might feel vulnerable or be manipulated, and make sure both of you respect each other's space. This will help protect your emotional well-being and prevent falling back into harmful dynamics.

Avoid Excessive Self-Criticism

Don't punish yourself for what may have gone wrong. Reflect on the relationship with the intention of learning, not blaming. Remember that everyone makes mistakes, and personal growth comes from self-compassion and understanding.

Surround Yourself With Positive Support

Seek people who provide emotional support and help you focus on the future. Talking to trusted friends or family can give you perspective and remind you that you're not alone in this process.

Engage in Activities That Strengthen You

Spend time on activities that you are passionate about or have always wanted to do. This will not only distract your mind but also help you reconnect with yourself and strengthen your sense of purpose.

Respect the Other Person's Process

Getting over a breakup involves recognizing that the other person also needs space and time to heal. Keep your distance when needed and avoid actions that could hinder both of your healing processes.

Focus on Your Well-Being

Take care of yourself, maintain healthy habits, and continue building the life you want, without neglecting your dreams and goals.

FINAL THOUGHTS

Getting over a breakup doesn't mean forgetting immediately or suppressing your feelings, but rather learning to live with them in a dignified and mature way, respecting both your own boundaries and those of the other person.

~~~

HOW TO KEEP A POSITIVE ATTITUDE DURING A BREAKUP: KEYS TO GETTING THROUGH IT WITH OPTIMISM

Going through a breakup is tough, and it's totally normal to feel sad, confused, and a bit lost. But keeping a positive attitude during this time is key to getting through it with resilience and finding your inner peace again. Here are some tips to help you stay hopeful and avoid getting stuck in negativity during this stage:

Accept Your Feelings Without Judging Them

The first step to staying positive is to accept that it's okay to feel bad after a breakup. Feeling sad, angry, or nostalgic is all part of the healing process. Accept these emotions without judging yourself or pressuring yourself to feel better right away. Every feeling has a purpose, and learning to live with them will help you heal faster.

Redefine Your Narrative

It's easy to fall into thoughts like "I'll never be happy again" or "I'll never find someone else." Change these negative beliefs into more realistic and hopeful affirmations, like "This pain will also pass" or "This is a chance to grow and get to know myself better." The way you talk to yourself shapes how you'll feel throughout this process.

Keep a Support System

Talking to friends, family, or even a professional can make a big difference. Surround yourself with people who value you, listen without judging, and remind you that you deserve to be happy. Sometimes, hearing other perspectives can help you see things in a less gloomy way.

Practice Gratitude

Even when things feel like they're falling apart, there are still little things to be grateful for. Take a few minutes each day to reflect on the good things you have (like a good friend, your health, or even a beautiful sunrise). Gratitude doesn't take away the pain, but it makes it more bearable and reminds you there's still beauty in life.

Spend Time on Yourself

Relationships can make us put aside our hobbies and personal goals. Use this time to reconnect with yourself. Exercise, start a new project, or get back into a hobby you used to love. Staying busy with activities that make you feel good not only boosts your mood but also helps you reconnect with yourself and rediscover what you're passionate about.

Visualize a Bright Future

It's hard to imagine a future without pain when you're grieving, but try to picture better days ahead. Life has a way of surprising us, and every breakup is also a chance for personal growth. Visualize moments of happiness, successes, and new connections—whether with others or with yourself.

FINAL THOUGHTS

Remember that everyone's healing process is different, and there's no magic formula to get over it. What matters most is taking care of yourself, being patient, and not losing hope. The pain will eventually turn into learning and growth.

~~~

WHAT NOT TO DO AFTER A BREAKUP: COMMON MISTAKES TO AVOID

Breakups are tough, and in the midst of the pain, we can make mistakes that make healing even harder without us realizing it. It's important to know what attitudes and behaviors to avoid so that you can heal in a healthy way and take your next steps toward personal growth. Here are some things you should steer clear of after a breakup.

Not Accepting the Breakup and Holding Onto False Hope

After a breakup, it's normal to want to hold onto the relationship, even when all signs show it's over. This attitude keeps you stuck in pain and needlessly drags out the suffering. It's key to accept what can't be changed and learn to let go.

Losing Your Self-Respect and Begging for Love

Sometimes, heartbreak can make us lose our self-respect, and we might be willing to do anything to get our ex back. This not only leads to rejection but also takes a toll on our self-esteem. Respect yourself enough not to beg or lower yourself in the process.

Jumping into Another Relationship Right Away

After a breakup, it might be tempting to jump straight into a new relationship to avoid feeling lonely or to fill the emptiness left by your ex. But it's important to give yourself time to heal and avoid making impulsive decisions that could make things worse. Taking some time to be alone lets you reflect, regain your balance, and start your next relationship from a healthier emotional place.

Idealizing the Past Relationship

It's easy to fall into the trap of idealizing the relationship that ended, remembering only the good times and ignoring why it ended. This kind of thinking not only keeps you stuck in the past but also makes it harder to move on. It's important to be realistic and remember both the good and the bad of the relationship.

Stalking Your Ex on Social Media

Keeping tabs on your ex's social media is a slippery slope. Seeing what they're up to or who they're with only adds to the pain and anxiety. The best move is to limit access to their profile or even block them temporarily to avoid temptation and focus on your own recovery.

Blaming Yourself for Everything

Breakups are rarely one person's fault. Blaming yourself entirely for everything that went wrong won't help you move forward. Instead, try to reflect on what happened, learn the lessons, and use them for personal growth. Self-compassion and forgiving yourself are key parts of this process.

Numbing the Pain with Substances or Rebound Relationships

Some people try to ease the pain by turning to alcohol, drugs, or jumping into new relationships impulsively. Although these might seem like quick fixes, they only delay healing and create more emotional issues. It's better to let yourself feel the pain and find healthier ways to deal with it.

Isolating Yourself Completely

Wanting some space after a breakup is normal, but isolating yourself from friends and loved ones can be harmful. Social support is crucial for emotional recovery. Talking to someone you trust, finding comfort in your close circle, and sharing what you're going through can make a huge difference in how you cope.

Making Important Decisions Impulsively

Strong emotions can make us want to make big changes—like moving, quitting a job, or making big purchases. However, it's best to put off major decisions until you're more emotionally stable. Impulsive decisions made in pain are usually fueled by temporary emotions and might not be the best choice.

Comparing Yourself to Your Ex's New Partner

If your ex is already in a new relationship, it's easy to compare yourself to their new partner and start doubting your worth. Remember that every person and relationship is unique, and what your ex does now has nothing to do with your value as a person. Avoiding these comparisons is key to protecting your self-esteem and emotional well-being.

Letting Yourself Be Controlled by Bitterness

Bitterness can lead to impulsive, harmful actions that make healing harder and hurt others in the process. Avoid doing things that could have serious consequences or go against your values. It's important to stay calm and find constructive ways to express your emotions.

FINAL THOUGHTS

Recovering from a breakup isn't always easy or straightforward, but avoiding these mistakes can make a huge difference in your emotional well-being. Every breakup is an opportunity to learn more about yourself, to grow, and to develop greater resilience. Give yourself permission to feel, to rest, and to seek help if you need it. Always remember that healing is possible and that you deserve peace and happiness again.

~~~

QUESTIONS TO ASK YOURSELF WHEN GOING THROUGH A BREAKUP: REFLECTING TO HEAL BETTER

Breakups can be painful and challenging, but they're also an opportunity for reflection and personal growth. Asking yourself some important questions during this time can help you understand your emotions better, figure out what you need, and start building a new life with more clarity and purpose. Here are some questions that might be helpful during this special time.

What hurts me the most about this breakup?

It's crucial to identify where your pain is coming from. Is it the loss of routine, the emotional connection, or the future you imagined together? Understanding what's really hurting helps you face your grief with more clarity and focus on healing those specific areas.

Am I being kind to myself?

During a breakup, it's easy to fall into self-criticism and blame yourself for everything that went wrong. Ask yourself if you're treating yourself with the compassion you deserve. Self-compassion is key to healing and moving forward without adding extra emotional weight to what you're already going through.

What can I learn from this experience?

Every relationship teaches us something, even when it ends. Reflecting on what you've learned about yourself, your needs, and your boundaries can help you grow and avoid repeating unhealthy patterns in the future.

What emotions am I avoiding?

Sometimes we avoid emotions like sadness, anger, or fear because they're uncomfortable. Ask yourself if there's anything you're pushing away. Feeling and processing these emotions is essential for letting them go and moving on in a healthy way.

What makes me feel better, even just a little bit?

Finding activities, people, or thoughts that bring you some comfort can be really helpful in managing the pain. It could be as simple as taking a walk, listening to music, or talking to a friend. Knowing what helps you can guide you to take concrete actions for self-care.

Am I idealizing the relationship I had?

It's common to idealize the relationship after a breakup and remember only the good times. Ask yourself if you're being realistic or if you're ignoring the difficulties that were there too. Having a balanced view of the relationship is important to let it go.

What are my boundaries now?

After a breakup, it's important to set clear boundaries—both with your ex and with yourself. Ask yourself what boundaries you need to protect your emotional well-being and make sure you're respecting your own needs.

What do I want for my future?

It can be hard to think about the future right after a breakup, but asking yourself what you want in the long run can help you set a new direction. This is a time to redefine your dreams and goals, and to remember that there are still plenty of things worth moving forward for.

Am I willing to ask for help if I need it?

Sometimes, we need support from friends, family, or even a professional to get through a breakup. Ask yourself if you're willing to reach out if the pain feels overwhelming. You don't have to go through this alone, and seeking support is a sign of strength.

What things make me feel grateful today?

Despite the pain, it's important to remember that there's always something to feel grateful for. Reflecting on what you still have in your life can help shift your focus and cultivate a more positive perspective, even in the middle of grief.

Am I allowing myself to rest?

It's important not to overburden yourself emotionally or physically. During a breakup, rest is essential to process the pain and maintain the energy needed for self-care.

Am I isolating myself from the people who care about me?

It's normal to want to be alone when you're going through tough times, but staying connected to friends and loved ones is vital for healing. Ask yourself if you're distancing yourself from those who can support you.

What behaviors am I using to avoid the pain?

Am I trying to fill the void with unhealthy behaviors, like excessive social media use, alcohol, or impulsive shopping? Identifying and replacing these behaviors with more positive actions is an important step toward recovery.

Am I only focusing on the negatives of the breakup?

Reflecting on the positive aspects and what you've learned from the relationship, even if it's tough, can help you get through it with a more open and balanced mindset.

What part of myself do I feel like I've lost?

Sometimes, a relationship can come to define a part of our identity. Ask yourself which aspects of yourself you feel you've lost, and start finding ways to reconnect with them or rediscover who you are without the relationship.

How can I use this time for personal growth?

Breakups can also be an opportunity to focus on projects, hobbies, or personal goals you had put aside. Ask yourself how you can use this moment to invest in yourself and grow in new ways.

Reflect and Connect with Yourself

These questions are an invitation to self-reflection and self-care. Take your time answering them honestly, and remember that every breakup, though painful, is also an opportunity for growth and transformation.

~~~

GLOSSARIES: KEY TERMS FOR UNDERSTANDING THE BREAKUP PROCESS

This glossary system is designed to help you navigate and better understand the breakup process. Each section addresses different aspects of the emotional, psychological, and relational journey, providing clear definitions that can help you identify and manage your feelings. Understanding these concepts is a crucial step toward healing and personal growth.

PSYCHOLOGICAL TERMS ABOUT BREAKUPS

This glossary is designed to help you understand how your mind works during a breakup. These concepts will help you identify and understand your emotions and thoughts, so you can heal and grow from this experience.

Acceptance: The stage in which you realize and accept that the relationship is over. Accepting reality is a key step to leaving the past behind and opening up to new opportunities in the future.

Catharsis: Releasing emotions by expressing how you feel deeply. It could be through crying, talking to someone, or doing something creative. Catharsis helps release tension and move toward healing.

Cognitive Dissonance: The feeling of inner conflict when you have two opposing thoughts. During a breakup, this might happen if one part of you knows the relationship wasn't good, but another part still wants to go back.

Cognitive Restructuring: A technique that involves identifying and changing negative or irrational thoughts to more positive and realistic ones. During a breakup, this can help you overcome limiting beliefs and recover in a healthier way.

Defense Mechanism: Strategies your mind uses without you realizing it to protect you from painful feelings. Examples during a breakup include denial, rationalization, and projection. These mechanisms can ease the initial emotional impact, but it's important to recognize them to avoid getting stuck.

Denial: A defense mechanism where you reject reality to avoid feeling distressed. After a breakup, denial might make it hard to accept that the relationship is over, which can delay the healing process.

Detachment: The process of emotionally letting go of someone. It doesn't mean you stop caring but learning to live without depending on that person for happiness. It's key to regaining emotional well-being after a breakup.

Emotional Dependence: The excessive need for someone else's support and validation to feel good about yourself. Emotional dependence can make getting over a breakup harder because you've lost both the relationship and your main source of security.

Introspection: Looking inward and reflecting on your thoughts, feelings, and actions. Introspection helps you understand what you feel, why you feel it, and how to move forward in a healthy and thoughtful way.

Projection: A defense mechanism where you put your own feelings, that you don't want to accept, onto someone else. During a breakup, you might blame your ex for feelings of guilt or anger that are really your own.

Rationalization: A defense mechanism where you come up with reasons to make a painful situation feel less bad. During a breakup, you might create explanations that make you feel better, even if they're not completely true. This can help ease the pain, but it doesn't always allow you to face reality.

Resilience: The ability to bounce back from tough situations. After a breakup, resilience helps you get through the pain, adapt to a new reality, and grow from the experience.

Self-Compassion: Being understanding and kind to yourself during tough times. After a breakup, self-compassion means treating yourself with the same care you would offer a friend in a similar situation.

Self-Confidence: Feeling sure of your abilities and strengths. After a breakup, your self-confidence may take a hit, but rebuilding it is crucial to moving forward and creating a fulfilling, independent life.

Separation Anxiety: The restless feeling that comes with the thought of being away from someone important. This is common after a breakup, especially if you shared a lot of your daily life with that person.

~~~

EMOTIONAL TERMS

This glossary is meant to help you identify and understand the emotions and feelings that come with a breakup. Each of these terms describes part of the emotional journey, providing context to help you normalize and process what you're going through.

Acceptance: The emotional state where we embrace the reality of the loss and start to integrate it into our life. Accepting doesn't mean forgetting, but learning to live with the absence and finding a new balance.

Anger: Intense frustration. It might be directed at yourself, your ex, or the situation in general, and it's a part of adjusting emotionally to the loss.

Anxiety: Restlessness and worry connected to fear or uncertainty about the future. During a breakup, anxiety can come from thinking about life without your partner or fearing loneliness. It can include repetitive thoughts and fear of not being able to handle the change.

Broken Hope: The feeling of disappointment when realizing that the dreams and plans we had can no longer happen. It's part of accepting reality.

Confusion: Emotional disorientation that happens when we experience mixed emotions, like love, anger, sadness, and hope all at once. This blend of feelings can make it hard to know what to do.
~~~

Grief: The emotional adaptation process after a significant loss. In a breakup, grief means dealing with the absence of your partner and rebuilding your life without them.

Guilt: The feeling of responsibility or regret for things we did or didn't do. In a breakup, guilt may come up when thinking about decisions or actions that might have contributed to the end of the relationship.

Heartache: The mix of resentment and sadness that can sometimes lead to wanting revenge. Heartache may push us to act impulsively or in unhealthy ways, like trying to hurt the other person. It's important to recognize this feeling and avoid acting on it to move forward in a healthy way.

Hope: A positive feeling that comes when we start seeing a future beyond the loss. Hope helps us focus on personal growth and new opportunities.

Hopelessness: A feeling of no positive expectations for the future. It's common in the early stages of grief, when it seems impossible to imagine life without that relationship.

Loneliness: The feeling of isolation after a breakup. It's important to tell the difference between being alone and feeling lonely, as loneliness can be eased by connecting with yourself and others.

Melancholy: Deep sadness connected to nostalgia for the good times. Melancholy often comes up when recalling the positive moments of the relationship.

Relief: A sense of peace that appears when a relationship full of conflict or tension ends. It might come along with sadness, but relief is a valid part of the healing process.

Resignation: A passive acceptance of the loss, which doesn't always lead to personal growth. Resignation can be a step before acceptance, but it's important to keep moving toward a state of learning.

Sadness: The sorrow and downheartedness we feel after a loss. It's a natural part of grief, and it helps us process the loss through emotional expression.

Vulnerability: Feeling exposed and insecure. During a breakup, vulnerability comes from accepting our feelings and sharing them with others, which is important for healing.

~~~

RELATIONAL TERMS

This glossary includes concepts related to relationship dynamics and how they impact breakups and the process afterward. Each of these terms will help you better understand different situations that can come up during a relationship and, eventually, during its end.

Amicable Breakup: A breakup where both partners accept the end of the relationship without major conflict. In an amicable breakup, both people understand that the relationship is no longer working but maintain respect and affection, allowing for a healthier, less painful separation.

Codependency: When someone is emotionally dependent on their partner to the point of losing their independence. In a codependent relationship, one person might feel like their happiness relies entirely on the other, leading to an imbalance and loss of personal identity.

Conflictive Breakup: A breakup that involves arguments, disagreements, and intense emotions. This type of breakup is often
~~~

painful and can leave deep emotional scars, making the healing process more difficult for both people.

Constructive Conflict: Disagreements or differences of opinion that, instead of hurting the relationship, make it stronger. Constructive conflict allows both people to express their needs and come to agreements, strengthening mutual understanding and emotional connection.

Emotional Dependence: Constantly needing validation and affection from your partner to feel good about yourself. Emotional dependence can make someone feel unable to be alone and constantly seek the other person's approval, which negatively affects both the relationship and personal well-being.

Emotional Manipulation: A strategy someone uses to control or influence the other's behavior, often using fear, guilt, or dependence. Emotional manipulation is a sign of a toxic relationship and can have very negative effects on the well-being of the person being manipulated.

Gaslighting: A form of manipulation where one person makes the other doubt their perception of reality. This behavior is harmful, as it can cause the victim to lose confidence in themselves and become emotionally dependent on the manipulator.

Healthy Detachment: The ability to emotionally let go of your partner without stopping loving them. Healthy detachment lets you keep your independence and well-being, avoiding excessive dependence while respecting personal boundaries.

Intimacy: A deep connection that involves emotional openness and vulnerability between partners. Intimacy is essential for a relationship to be fulfilling and long-lasting, and it's built through trust, respect, and honest communication.

Mutual Support Relationship: A relationship where both people support each other in their personal goals and challenges. This type of relationship is based on respect, communication, and the desire to see the other grow and be happy, and it's crucial for both partners' well-being.

On-and-Off Relationship: A relationship with frequent breakups and reconciliations. This kind of relationship can be emotionally exhausting, as both partners get caught in a cycle of breaking up and getting back together, which makes it hard to find stability and emotional growth.

Personal Boundaries: Emotional and physical limits someone sets to protect their well-being. Personal boundaries are crucial for keeping respect and independence in a relationship. Setting and communicating these boundaries helps both people feel safe and valued.

Rebound Relationship: A relationship that starts soon after a breakup, often to avoid the pain of separation. Rebound relationships are usually short-lived and don't always allow people to properly process the grief from their previous relationship.

Reconciliation: The process of trying to restore a relationship after a breakup. Reconciliation can happen when both people recognize the problems that caused the breakup and are willing to work on them to rebuild the relationship on healthier grounds.

Toxic Relationship: A relationship where one or both partners show harmful behaviors that affect the other's well-being. Toxic relationships are often full of manipulation, disrespect, and unbalanced power dynamics, preventing both people from growing emotionally.

~~~
~~~

TYPES OF RELATIONSHIPS AND BREAKUPS

This glossary is designed to help readers identify the type of relationship they had and understand how that affects their grieving process. Understanding the nature of the relationship can make the healing journey easier since every type of relationship and breakup comes with its own challenges and lessons.

Abusive Relationship: A relationship where one person has power and control over the other, often through emotional, physical, or psychological abuse. Breaking free from an abusive relationship can be especially hard because abuse creates fear and dependence. However, leaving an abusive relationship is the first step toward healing and rebuilding self-esteem.

Amicable Breakup: A breakup where both people agree to end the relationship without major conflict. An amicable breakup is characterized by mutual respect and understanding, and it tends to be less painful than other breakups since both people agree it's the best choice for them. Still, there may be feelings of sadness and nostalgia.

Breakup for Personal Growth: A breakup that happens because one or both people feel they've grown in different directions and the relationship no longer supports their well-being or personal development. This kind of breakup, while painful, can be an opportunity for both people to keep growing independently.

Casual Relationship: A relationship without long-term commitment, where both people want to enjoy the present without future expectations. Breaking up from a casual relationship can be less painful, though it might be tough if one person developed deeper feelings.

Codependent Relationship: A relationship where both people depend on each other emotionally in an unhealthy way. Each person tries to meet their own needs through the other, creating a cycle of dependence that's hard to break. The breakup of a codependent relationship means learning to meet your own needs without relying on the other person.

Conflictive Breakup: A breakup that involves intense disagreements and arguments. This type of breakup leaves deeper emotional wounds because of the conflict and the harm caused during the process. The grieving process after a conflictive breakup can take more time and require a conscious effort to let go of resentment and anger.

Dependent Relationship: A relationship where one person depends on the other to meet their emotional needs. In this kind of relationship, one or both people might feel like they can't live without the other. Breaking up from a dependent relationship can be difficult since it involves regaining independence and learning to find happiness without constant validation from the other person.

Ghosting: Ending a relationship abruptly and without any communication, which can cause confusion and hurt for the person experiencing it since they're left without answers or emotional closure.

Long-Distance Relationship: A relationship where partners live far apart and don't get to see each other in person often. This type of relationship requires a lot of commitment and mutual trust. The breakup of a long-distance relationship can bring a specific kind of pain related to the lack of contact and the struggle to keep the connection over time.

Mutual Breakup: A breakup where both people agree that ending the relationship is for the best. While it may be less traumatic than other breakups, it's still painful since both people are losing a meaningful connection, but they do so with the certainty that it's the right decision.

Mutual Support Relationship: A relationship where both people support each other in their goals and personal challenges. Even though these relationships are usually healthy, when they end, the grieving process can mean losing not just a partner but also an important companion and source of support.

On-and-Off Relationship: A relationship characterized by constant breakups and reconciliations. This type of relationship can be emotionally draining because the back-and-forth creates insecurity and makes it hard to build a stable connection. Finally ending an on-and-off relationship can be a relief, but it also comes with the challenge of breaking the cycle and accepting that it's time to stop trying to get back together.

Rebound Relationship: A relationship that starts soon after a breakup, often to fill the emotional void left by the previous one. Rebound relationships are usually a way to avoid facing the pain of a breakup, and while they sometimes evolve into something more stable, they often end when the person feels ready to be alone again.

Short-Term Relationship: A relationship that doesn't last long, usually without getting too serious. The breakup of a short-term relationship is often less painful, but it can still leave feelings of "what if" or doubts about what could have happened if more effort had been made.

Toxic Relationship: A relationship where one or both people show behaviors that harm the other's emotional or physical well-being. Toxic relationships are often marked by manipulation, disrespect, and control. Breaking free from a toxic relationship can be very liberating, but it can also leave emotional scars that require time and support to heal.

Unexpected Breakup: A breakup that happens suddenly for one or both people. Unexpected breakups are especially painful because of the lack of emotional preparation and the feeling of sudden loss. This type of breakup may create a stronger need for answers and explanations to help accept the situation.

~~~

TECHNIQUES AND STRATEGIES FOR HEALING

This glossary includes terms related to techniques and strategies you can use during your healing journey. Each of these practices is designed to help you manage your emotions, reduce stress, and promote personal growth after a breakup.

Cognitive Reappraisal: A technique of reinterpreting a situation to change its emotional impact. Cognitive reappraisal lets you shift how you see a painful situation, finding a positive meaning or lesson in the experience. This helps reduce the pain and move forward in a healthier way.

Connecting with Nature: Spending time outdoors to connect with nature, which can have a calming and refreshing effect. Walking in a park, listening to birds, or simply being surrounded by nature can help reduce stress and improve your overall well-being.

Deep Breathing: A technique involving slow, controlled breathing that helps reduce anxiety and stress. Practicing deep breathing can help you relax during moments of distress, calming your nervous system and promoting a sense of peace.

Gratitude Practice: Focusing on the positive things in your life and being thankful for them. Gratitude helps shift your focus from what's missing or lost to what you still have and value, improving your perspective and emotional state.
~~~

Journaling: The practice of regularly writing about your thoughts, emotions, and experiences to better process them. Keeping a journal allows you to explore your feelings more deeply and reflect on your emotional progress over time.

Meditation: A relaxation and focus technique that helps manage anxiety and stress. Meditation lets you focus on your breathing and the present moment, helping calm the mind and reduce negative thoughts that often arise during a breakup.

Mindfulness: The practice of being present in the current moment without judging the emotions that arise. Mindfulness helps you accept what you're feeling without trying to change or avoid it. This practice is especially helpful for reducing anxiety and preventing negative thoughts from taking over.

Physical Exercise: Physical activity that releases endorphins, also known as the "happiness hormones." Exercise not only improves your physical state but is also an excellent tool for releasing tension, reducing anxiety, and boosting your mood.

Positive Affirmations: Positive phrases that you repeat to change negative thinking patterns. Affirmations like "I am enough" or "I deserve to be happy" help reprogram your mind and cultivate a more positive and empowering attitude.

Positive Visualization: A technique of imagining positive situations or desired outcomes to reduce stress and increase well-being. Visualizing yourself overcoming the pain and feeling happy can motivate you and help you maintain a more optimistic attitude as you navigate the grieving process.

Progressive Muscle Relaxation: A method that involves tensing and then relaxing different muscle groups to reduce physical and mental tension. This technique is helpful for releasing built-up stress in the body and relaxing the mind.

Self-Care: A set of actions and habits aimed at taking care of your physical and mental health. Self-care means doing things that make you feel good, like resting, eating well, exercising, and spending time on activities you enjoy. Practicing self-care is crucial for regaining your well-being after a breakup.

Social Support: Reaching out for and accepting support from friends, family, or support groups who can offer understanding and empathy. Talking with trusted people about what you're experiencing can lighten the emotional load and give you a sense of belonging and connection during the grieving process.

Talk Therapy: Talking with a therapist to explore and process the emotions from a breakup. Therapy provides a safe space to express your feelings, identify patterns that make healing harder, and gain effective tools to face the grieving process.

Therapeutic Writing: Using writing to express emotions and let go of emotional tension. Writing about how you feel, whether in a journal or in letters you never send, is an effective way to process and release accumulated emotions, helping you clarify your thoughts and better understand your feelings.

~~~

BIBLIOGRAPHY

– Castillo Cañadas A. AGRUPAR: Guided Help for Relationship Breakup. Group intervention program to reduce negative consequences of romantic breakup in young adults aged 18 to 24 [Internet]. 2022 [cited 2024 Aug 18]. Available from: https://dspace.umh.es/handle/11000/27842

– Castillo Trelles GO, Rabanal Rimaycuna AE. Grief over romantic breakups among psychology students in the first and final cycles of a private university in Piura, 2023 [Internet]. 2024 [cited 2024 Oct 1]. Available from: https://repositorio.upao.edu.pe/handle/20.500.12759/35371

– Collazos Ticona GR. Posttraumatic growth and emotional regulation after a romantic breakup [Internet]. 2022 [cited 2024 Aug 24]. Available from: https://tesis.pucp.edu.pe/repositorio/handle/20.500.12404/22880

– Dantas Guedes D. From falling in love to going through grief over romantic breakup: considerations based on attachment theory, psychoanalysis, and psychoneurology. RPP [Internet]. 2022 May 23 [cited 2024 Oct 8];(5). Available from: http://p3.usal.edu.ar/index.php/psicol/article/view/5991

– Garabito S, García FE, Neira M, Puentes E. Relationship breakup in young adults and mental health: coping strategies for the stress of ending a relationship. Psychologia. Advances in Discipline [Internet]. 2020 [cited 2024 Aug

30];14(1):47-59. Epub 2021 Jan 26. Available from: https://doi.org/10.21500/19002386.4560

– Guedes D. Mediation of attachment representations in coping with the experience of romantic relationship breakup. Rev Cient Arbit Fund MenteClara [Internet]. 2022 Dec [cited 2024 Aug 15];7. Available from: https://fundacionmenteclara.org.ar/revista/index.php/RCA/article/view/315 doi: https://doi.org/10.32351/rca.v7.315

– Gutiérrez Flores A. Emotional affective dependence, stress levels, and coping strategies in students of the Psychology program at Universidad Mayor de San Andrés [Internet]. 2022 [cited 2024 Oct 5]. Available from: https://repositorio.umsa.bo/handle/123456789/29330

– Henao Ceballos P, Muñoz Y. Analysis of coping with romantic breakups from the perspective of consumer psychology. Diversitas Perspect Psicol [Internet]. 2021 [cited 2024 Sep 25];17(2):151-161. Epub 2021 Jul 1. Available from: https://doi.org/10.15332/22563067.7110

– Manrique Bustos AM, Miranda Giraldo J. Discourse analysis of four participants experiencing romantic breakup based on acceptance and commitment theory [Internet]. 2023 [cited 2024 Sep 3]. Available from: https://alejandria.poligran.edu.co/handle/10823/6997

– Mateo Crisóstomo Y, Aguilar Zavala H, Arméndariz García NA, García Campos ML, Hernández Ramírez G. Coping strategies for stress in young drug users: integrative review. Ciencia Latina [Internet]. 2023 Aug 3 [cited 2024

Aug 19];7(4):2477-93. Available from: https://ciencialatina.org/index.php/cienciala/article/view/7068

– Mendoza D, Guzmán-Saldaña RM, Lerma-Talamantes A, Bosques–Brugada LE. Romantic breakup, grief process, and academic aspects in university students. ICSA [Internet]. 2021 Dec 5 [cited 2024 Aug 22];10(19):9-16. Available from: https://repository.uaeh.edu.mx/revistas/index.php/ICSA/article/view/7967

– Navarro Vásquez P. Online group intervention for grief processing and psychological well-being recovery after a romantic breakup. Ciencia y Sociedad [Internet]. 2020 [cited 2024 Oct 22];45(4):119-132. Available from: https://doi.org/10.22206/cys.2020.v45i4.pp119-132

– Peñuñuri LY, Rey-Anacona CA, Suárez YB. Therapeutic treatments for coping with romantic breakup: A systematic review. Psychologia. Advances in Discipline [Internet]. 2024 [cited 2024 Oct 17];18(1):23-37. Epub 2024 Oct 3. Available from: https://doi.org/10.21500/19002386.6577

– Ramos Sánchez AR, Alzola Rivera M. Resilience in young people after romantic breakup [Internet]. 2023 [cited 2024 Aug 31]. Available from: https://riull.ull.es/xmlui/handle/915/33907

– Seales Rodríguez E. Grief in romantic breakup [Internet]. Medellín and Envigado: Universidad Cooperativa de Colombia, Faculty of Social Sciences, Psychology; 2024. Available from: https://hdl.handle.net/20.500.12494/56847

~~~

Don't miss out!

Visit the website below and you can sign up to receive emails whenever Arturo José Sánchez Hernández publishes a new book. There's no charge and no obligation.

https://books2read.com/r/B-A-RZZWB-SPIGF

BOOKS 2 READ

Connecting independent readers to independent writers.

Did you love *When Love Ends*? Then you should read *Keys to Effective Seduction*[1] by Arturo José Sánchez Hernández!

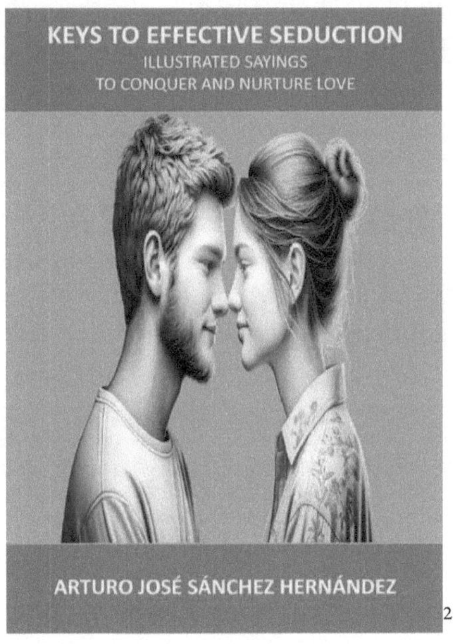

[2]

An innovative combination of sayings and images to guide the reader in the art of conquering and maintaining a successful romantic relationship. Throughout six chapters, key topics are addressed, such as overcoming irrational thoughts that hinder courtship, interpreting sexual signals, and developing essential qualities to spark and sustain sexual and emotional interest in a partner. From the importance of verbal and non-verbal communication to the ability to choose or reject whom to court, the book offers practical and thoughtful guidance that emphasizes self-control and responsibility in courtship. Additionally, it includes general tips for seduction, a compilation of Cuban compliments and sayings, and a glossary of relevant terms. With its

---

1. https://books2read.com/u/3LE1rM

2. https://books2read.com/u/3LE1rM

unique approach that blends tradition and technology, this work not only instructs but also inspires and motivates readers on their journey toward a fulfilling and lasting romantic relationship.

Also by Arturo José Sánchez Hernández

Adolescentes con Propósito
Propósito en Marcha

Detti illustrati
Virtù cardinali
Chiavi per sedurre con efficacia

Dictons illustrés
Vertus Cardinals
Clés Pour Séduire Efficacement
Attitudes Puissantes
Décide avec Sagesse

Ditados Ilustrados
Virtudes Cardinais
Chaves Para Conquistar Com Eficácia

Guérison et croissance personnelle

Quand l'amour s'achève

Healing and Personal Growth

When Love Ends

Challenging Loneliness

Rebirth Behind Bars

Illustrated sayings

Cardinal Virtues

Keys to Effective Seduction

Powerful Attitudes

Decide Wisely

Jugendliche mit Zweck

Zweck in Aktion

Sanación y Crecimiento Personal

Cuando el Amor Termina

Desafiando la Soledad

Renacer entre Rejas

Teens with Purpose

Purpose in Action

About the Author

Arturo José Sánchez Hernández, born in Havana in 1970, is a physician specializing in Comprehensive General Medicine and Psychiatry. He has an extensive professional and academic background, supported by several publications focused on ethics and the theory of values.

With notable experience in sexuality and couple and family psychotherapy, Dr. Sánchez Hernández has devoted part of his career to exploring these areas of mental health. Additionally, he is distinguished as an author of self-help and personal growth books, where sayings and images play a central role.

He currently resides in Maun, Botswana, where he practices as a psychiatrist at the Letsholathebe II Memorial Hospital. His commitment to mental health and individual well-being has made him a highly regarded professional both in his home country and in his new community in Botswana.

www.ingramcontent.com/pod-product-compliance
Lightning Source LLC
LaVergne TN
LVHW041121150826
845673LV00007B/2149

* 9 7 9 8 2 3 0 3 8 1 1 4 3 *